*Your Marriage*

# CLASSIC OR CLUNKER

**Connie Bellemere, MA/LMHC**

Sound Counseling Press

Published in the United States by Sound Counseling Press

10  9  8  7  6  5  4  3  2  1
ISBN: 978-0-615-52043-8

The self-help resources in this book are not intended to be a substitute for therapy or professional advice. Any reference to people or cases are a composite or altered identity used only as illustration.

For information about special discounts for bulk purchases or to book the author for your live event contact www.soundcounseling.net.

Bellemere, Connie

Your Marriage:  Classic or Clunker

1. Marriage  2. Marriage maintenance manual  3.Relationship skills

*Dedicated to*
*The colossal courage and curiosity*
*of couples in counseling.*
*Your devotion inspired this handbook.*
*Thank you for allowing me to*
*be a guide on your ride.*

# TABLE OF CONTENTS

# TABLE OF CONTENTS CONTINUED

# ACKNOWLEDGEMENTS

*My heartfelt thanks go to the following:*

*My friends and family for their constant positivity and support, the fuel that helped me keep on trucking over the past several years. I know that they rally around me as I finally get this book on the road.*

*Lloyd Axelrod for his unrelenting belief, talent, and expert assistance. His kindness and encouragement drove me onward.*

*Lori Stephens, Verbatim Editorial, for not only catching grammar glitches but also for steering me in the right direction and keeping me on course. Her steady urging and purging significantly improved the quality of my work.*

*Tharon Knittle, TK Branding, for graphic design work that helped the spirit of the book come alive. Her collaboration, abundance of patience, and enthusiasm made the journey delightful.*

# INTRODUCTION

*Your car (relationship)*
*does not make you happy.*
*It is the vehicle in which you*
*chose to experience life.*

Remember your first car? It might not have been the most expensive, shiny, or newest car, but it was yours.

I remember mine. I was 17 and couldn't wait to leave home. I was waitressing at a "fine diner" (the W. T. Grant Department Store) in Lewiston, Idaho to earn money to go to college. It was there that I met and befriended Claudette, the eccentric French chef.

1

When I disclosed my desire for freedom to Claudette, she said she had just the thing to help me get started: a car she wanted to sell. If I came by her house, she'd show it to me. I thought a car definitely seemed like the answer to all my problems. Later, at her house, she took me to her backyard, and there was my car, wrenched up into a tree by a seven-foot chain. She lowered it and brought it to the driveway for me to inspect.

With the vast experience a 17-year-old girl has with cars, I "ooood" and "aaahed" over the glossy, black, four-door 1949 Chevy. It was love at first sight! My mind was ablaze with the fun, freedom, and happiness the car would bring me. To this day, I feel good when I think of that car.

More importantly, it was dirt cheap; $45.00. I was thrilled at my deal and all it represented, and I drove it home to present to my parents.

My dad was excited. Knowing significantly more than I did about cars, he inspected it thoroughly and reported that it was in remarkable mechanical condition, which confirmed for me how smart I was to buy it. The next week, he and I were under the hood, giving it a tune up.

The following week, my parents informed me that because I now owned a car, I would also have to buy insurance, and I learned how much insurance cost—$150—which I really couldn't afford.

Two weeks later, I had a flat. Dad told me I should get a new tire, which I did. It cost $50—five dollars more than the car!

The romance was off for this car-ownership deal. I thought a car would bring me freedom and happiness, and it did for a few weeks. I didn't consider that I would have to also pay for insurance, gas, tires, oil, and tune ups. Where was I going to get a chain and a tree at college?

Buying a new car is like beginning a new relationship. The rush of excitement is intoxicating! There is so much promise in what a car can potentially offer, especially for the young and uninitiated. There's the new-car smell and countless options. Today cars are technological miracles. They have automatic antennas, air conditioning, GPS systems, automatic door openers, heated seats, and even seats that automatically adjust for the driver's body.

When you own your own car, you learn that these features are not without flaws. Cars break down. Parts need to be fixed and replaced.

Nonetheless, no one is ready to go back to the horse and buggy days. Our metal, multi-optioned marvels are here to stay.

## The "Happily Ever After" Myth

I'd like you to meet Slick Willie, the car salesman. "Yeah, this car will be the last car you will ever need. You'll love this car! It is virtually maintenance free, rarely needs gas, and the tires will last forever. See, there isn't even a spare tire, lug wrench, or jack in the back. Yes, siree, buy this car, and you'll drive happily ever after."

I hope you're laughing. And yet, on some level, isn't that the story we buy regarding marriage? How many fairy tales and movies end with some version of "and they lived happily ever after"?

As a kid, I loved those stories (though I certainly wasn't living in a fairyland in my house). Yet, the promise was that if I just found a prince of a guy, he'd marry me and, through our pure love, we would love each other forever!

Hope springs eternal when two people marry. There is such courage and idealism that, despite all the statistics on divorce, they believe that with their special intelligence, love, and innate wisdom, they will live happily ever after.

If you imagine this young couple as new drivers, it's most likely that they never earned learner's permits, read through warranties, bought any insurance or a tool kit, or reviewed an owner's manual.

I work as a counselor, and some of my most rewarding work has been with couples who need help for some type of relationship breakdown. They really love each other—or did at one time—but have noticed that things aren't working that well. They want to find out what's wrong and how to fix the problems in their relationship. They believe that a fulfilling relationship is possible and are ready to do whatever it takes to get their marriage back on the road. They are begging for tools and understanding of how to make it all work.

Their pleading, pain, courage, and hard work inspired me to write this manual. I wanted to provide sound, easily understood information on the mechanics of marriage and give some basic tools that couples can use for maintenance and repairs. My desire is to help them put the joy of the journey back into their relationship.

Marriage won't make you happy all the time, but it can be a helluva ride!

As you think about how your car works and the effort it takes to maintain it, it is clear that we need a "manual" for our relationships. Most people can handle the simple maintenance and minor breakdowns in a relationship, but for the more difficult breakdowns or accidents, you probably need a qualified "mechanic" (counselor). You know that it is less costly to prevent problems and treat minor problems than to let things deteriorate to the point where the engine of your relationship needs a complete overhaul.

This manual is filled with basic action items that YOU can do to prevent breakdowns and accidents while maintaining the rich and rewarding journey of your relationship. You can influence the destiny of your marriage. While you can't always control what happens to you on the journey, you can control how you respond to what happens. Your perception, attitude, and willingness to learn as much as possible about the care of your marriage is up to you.

If you have a car and want to keep it on the road, you know that you are responsible for its' upkeep.

You have to know how it works, not just how to drive it. While your relationship did not come with a manual, THIS manual provides you with valuable information about the features, operations, maintenance requirements at various stages, and other vital information.

This manual is a reference for optimal operation in your marriage. Keep it handy!

# THE ROADMAP

A roadmap is the most important tool in the tool bag of your relationship. Once you have it, you can both create a mental picture of where you want to go.

All new ventures begin with possibility thinking, not probability thinking. Probabilities are based on evidence that is strong enough to support a presumption. Possibilities are not. Success-driven, focused people assume that anything is possible. It's this belief that sustains them through the difficult times. This type of mindset means holding onto an ideal and unique image of the future for the common good. It implies a choice of values and actions that bring meaning and purpose to our lives.

Creating a clear mental image is paramount in a world in which we are constantly bombarded by distractions. If we don't have a clear image of our hopes, dreams, and aspirations, there is little chance that we will muster the energy and effort to make them happen.

Start with a clear idea of what's important to you, who you are, and who you want to be. Without this type of clarity, other people, things, and situations will determine your future.

You may have to negotiate about what you want to do along the way or how to get there, but once you set the agenda, you gather purpose and ignite the passion of preparation and anticipation. You begin to believe that what's merely a shared image can be made real. Together, you can decide what is worthy and meaningful in your lives.

# Staying on Course

When we feel passionately about the kind of world we want for ourselves and others, we are more motivated and committed to take action.

If you don't feel deeply about something or someone, how can you expect others to feel a sense of commitment? How can you expect another person to feel jazzed and excited if you don't? How can you expect another person to suffer though the hard work and sacrifice necessary to create a dream if you don't?

Suffering and hard work? You may think, "Wait a minute, that's not what I signed up for. Why would I want this?" Suffering and hard work are directly tied in to your passion for something (or someone). When you have passionate, juicy goals, you get a passionate, juicy life.

Look up "passion" up in the dictionary: you will see that it relates to suffering. Life requires a certain amount of hard work and suffering all on its own, but you can choose to live with passion or a hum-drum existence. If you choose passion, you must have a goal for which you are willing.

## Are We There Yet? The Answer Is No

I often see couples who are stuck in the grief of attachment to perfectionism—especially in regard to their partner's imperfections. I asked one woman to write down all the concerns she had with her husband. She brought me a legal pad with 10 pages of notes about all his imperfections! I was so over-whelmed that I'm not sure I let her finish reading it all.

I said, "Stop. You're all over the map and backseat driving, going so many different directions that your partner is lost in a fog." I handed her a 3x5 card and said, "I'd like you to write down three things that you want from your husband. Use the phrasing I want, not I don't want. Keep your ideas simple, positive, and in the present tense. What is your true vision for your relationship? List only the three most im-portant issues. In the future, whenever you have a conflict with your husband, discuss only what you have written on the card."

*Perfectionism doesn't believe in practice shots. It doesn't believe in improvement. ...Perfectionism thrives on comparison and competition. It doesn't know how to say, "good try" or "job well done." The critic does not believe in creative glee—or any glee at all, for that matter. No, perfectionism is a serious matter.*
*-- Julia Cameron, "Finding Water"*

Months later, she called to thank me, saying, "I told my husband clearly and simply what I wanted, instead of just criticizing him; we are both much happier. Now he has changed so much!" Her husband really did want a happy wife. When he no longer heard long lists of criticism, he no longer had to be defensive and could hear her needs in a new way.

In other counseling cases, one partner may plead, "But you don't understand. We've been coming here for six weeks, and my wife still doesn't do what I want." I will ask, "Has there been any movement in that direction?" If the client says, "No," then I ask, "Is that true?" The client is likely to say, "Well, no, but it's very little. How can I help her if I don't criticize her?"

Change happens in small, incremental steps. When people are just beginning to change their habits, they need a lot more encouragement than criticism. Most of us want to please a loved one. We smile when we know that what we did is pleasing to them. We endlessly cheer a baby's first steps, successful potty chair training, and attempts at tying shoes and riding a bike. We say, "WOW, good job! Look at that! I'm so impressed." The child's face lights up.

Speeding to your ultimate destination certainly does not make for an enjoyable ride. What IS your ultimate destiny, anyway?

Perfectionism forces people to:

- be continually dissatisfied

- constantly focus on what isn't working

- create a suspicious, tense, frustrating atmosphere

- nitpick at the negative

- measure everything by some mysterious and impossible standard

- lack appreciation, praise, generosity, and encouragement

- never attain contentment

- rarely feel pride in themselves or the relationship

Perfectionism is a cruel and perpetually dissatisfied master.

# LOOK Under the Hood

## 7 Point Inspection for Perfectionism

What happened when you made a mistake as a child?

1. How did your mother react?

2. How did your father react?

3. How did you feel?

4.  What did you learn about mistakes?

5.  Write about a time when you were totally and enjoyably enveloped in the joy of learning. Describe the elements of:

    • Play-

    • Exploration-

    • Adventure-

    • Curiosity-

• Being in tune-

6. Did anyone cheer you on? If so, who was it?

# SAFETY FIRST

## Driver's Education

Today, an abundance of information is available on how to create a classic car—or a stellar marriage. Don't wait until your car (or relationship) breaks down or is in dire need of repair. Immerse yourself in learning now!

The problem with today's marriages is that people are trying to design relationships with outdated tools—tools inherited from our parents who inherited them from their parents, and so on. This is like trying to design a Boeing 747 with a slide rule[1]. At one time that was exactly what was needed; now airplane designs are computer-generated. The old tools must be reinvented. The problem isn't in the institution of marriage; it is that in this rapidly changing world, we cannot afford to use outdated instruments and designs. New tools are essential to compete in today's world.

Hone your curiosity. Discover how things work well (including how your partner "works"). Your abilities to tune into and work with your partner are key to the quality of your ride.

You must be the innovator in your marriage. Innovators are curious and see mistakes as opportunities. The Wright Brothers ran through farm fields with fabricated wings harnessed to their backs. Consider the lives of people like Walt Disney and Bill Gates. These are people who believed in their ideas, no matter what the odds. No business would ever get off the ground if its founders listened to the statistics about new businesses!

---

1 A manual calculating device consisting of two rulers marked with graduated scales, one sliding against the other.

## Safety Precautions

No one wants to be a crash-test dummy while driving their car. Even before we get into a car, we want to know that precautionary construction, safety, and design features are in place for a secure ride. Should an accident happen, we want to know that our automobile was engineered to minimize the possibility of injury and death.

What that means to a relationship is that growth and intimacy can occur only in a secure environment. In marriages where there are frequent threats of divorce or suicide (i.e., totaling the car), there is not enough safety to move forward. In other situations, when one partner gets scared and jumps out of the car ("I'm leaving" or has an affair), again, assurance of a smooth ride is impossible. There may be other more subtle behaviors that threaten your relationship.

# LOOK Under the Hood

1. What makes you feel safe in a relationship?


2. What makes you feel unsafe?


3. Who in your past made you feel unsafe? What behaviors or demeanors led you to feel unsafe?


4. How are these unresolved fears from the past impacting your current relationship?

5.  What measures have you taken to rid yourself of these fears?

6.  What do you do when you get afraid?

7.  What do you do when your partner gets afraid?

8.  Is it safe to show your vulnerable side with your partner? Why or why not?

# SYSTEMS

## Fuel

Communication is the "gasoline" and life blood of your relationship. Couples in long-standing, healthy marriages are able to resolve the conflicts and "breakdowns" that are inevitable in any relationship. They know that "happily ever after" is a myth.

The greatest challenge in communication is to first define the ISSUE and stick with just one issue.

Once that is done, you can move on to these five parts:

- Perceptions: the five senses (see, hear, taste, smell, touch)

- Interpretations: beliefs, interpretations, judgments, speculations

- Feelings: glad, mad, sad, discounted, hurt, happy, frightened

- Intention: wants stated in the positive

- Action

Arguments are sustained when people try to convince each other their perceptions and interpretations are right or wrong. "Did so!" "Did not!" "That's a ridiculous belief." This is a head-to-head connection.

Attending to your partner's feelings and wants with curiosity (versus judgment) will lead to a heart-to-heart connection and desired intimacy.

## Are You Listening or Reloading?

Listening is even more important than "talking," which many confuse with communication. Amaze the speaker with your understanding of his or her experience.

Reflective listening acknowledges that you understand the speaker's message and feelings behind the message. Suggested techniques include the following:

- Clarify (Ask open-ended questions )

- Restate

- Summarize

- Validate

- Encourage ("Tell me more.")

Listening includes nonverbal feedback as well. This may include:

- Maintaining eye contact

- Leaning slightly forward

- Using an arms-open stance

Think of the times when you felt really understood or misunderstood by someone. What verbal and nonverbal feedback caused you to feel understood?

## Fuel Efficiency

How you drive and maintain your car will determine effective fuel consumption or communication. Follow these hints for better motoring.

- Avoid short, sharp startups; gently accelerate from a rest.

- Don't start your conversation with a sudden burst of energy when you know the topic is sensitive.

- Use the appropriate gear.

- Use low gears (soft and slow voice and volume) for hills and save the higher gears for freeway driving.

- Anticipate obstructions and adjust your speed well in advance.

- Have a "deceleration" plan for those times when intensity seems eminent.

- Don't gun the engine.

*Harsh start-up—that is, beginning with criticism or contempt—causes the interaction to go downhill fast. Partners become defensive and withdraw, leading to emotional distanced and loneliness. The opposite is softened, start-up which is free of criticism and contempt.*
*-- John Gottman*

Comments like "If he loved me, he'd know what I want" or "If you love each other, it's easy" signal an accident waiting to happen.

Marriages are crucibles in which we continuously try to learn to connect intimately to another human being. Each of us invites into our inner circle mentors and tormentors—sometimes they are one in the same. Often we learn more from tormentors as pain is such a great motivator to learning.

Communication, love, respect, and care are the lubricant that keeps the car going smoothly. Gasoline keeps a car running, and dirty fuel and unnecessary additives impact the car's entire performance system. Communication is the "gasoline" of your relationship. Keep the tank full, and use the proper octane!

## Steering

I've had more than one client challenge me by saying, "With all the divorces, why would I want to get married (in the car) in the first place?"

Hopefully you will never have an accident or a fender bender but you can successfully learn how to drive your car (your relationship). This manual provides you with the tools you need.

Others try to avoid error by staying in familiar territory. Life is so short. The world so vast that I feel safe in saying that if once you learn the basics, with increased awareness (especially of patterns in interaction) and steady practice you can become an increasingly good driver and go on many adventurous journeys.

More apt questions include, "Are we headed in the right direction?" and "What are we focusing on?" Expert drivers know where to focus.

## Braking

In 2009, 500,000 Toyota Priuses were recalled because there was a flaw in the software that makes the brakes momentarily unresponsive. We can't "recall" our human software, but we can reprogram it.

When some couples hit a "bumpy" or "slippery" place in their relationship, the tension compels one or both to "accelerate" and increase the intensity, even to the point where the intensity (the accelerator pedal) seems stuck. Some drivers are in a constant state of road rage. Little things bug them A LOT!! They are impatient, irritated, angry, demanding and rude. It's like they are always accelerating and their accelerator pedal is always stuck.

In this case, slowing down and pulling off to the side of the road is the most effective way to manage the acceleration.

In a relationship, sudden and extreme acceleration feels out of control and scary, and it can lead to a rapid deterioration of the relationship. Remember to take your foot off the accelerator and put on the brakes when things get intense.

## Cooling

*Keeping the cooling system in good shape will go a long way toward keeping you cool when things heat up on the road.*
*-- Auto Repair for Dummies*

The cooling system of a car gets rid of excess heat. If not properly dispelled, excess heat can cause anything from an inconvenient breakdown to severe engine damage. Only about 25% of this heat is used by the engine for combustion. About 35% passes out through the exhaust system, and 10% is lost to internal friction and the lubrication system.

The remaining heat is carried away by the cooling system.

Your engine temperature can creep up to 1,000 degrees Fahrenheit! Knowing this, it is easy to see that you are headed for a major meltdown without taking certain important precautions. If the cooling system doesn't work, the lubricating oil can evaporate, and parts can seize or melt. In short, the engine is fried.

## The Temperature Gauge: Maintaining Your Cool

In a relationship, you need a gauge to maintain an optimal "temperature" or intensity of connectivity. During a conversation, rate the intensity of your encounter on a scale from 1 to 10, 10 being a heated debate.

At levels 8, 9, and 10, you are in the equivalent of the red zone on the temperature gauge of your car and headed for a major engine failure. In this zone, there is a fiery maelstrom of explosive anger, rapid mood swings, suspiciousness, unrealistic expectations, to which nobody is listening. With your pedal to the metal, you are a not so wreck less speeder. Your car is unsafe. Pull over, stop, and wait for things to cool down for at least twenty minutes.

A major cause of overheating between partners is shoulding, telling yourself that you have an obligation to do something differently from what you are doing. Psychologist Albert Ellis calls it "musterba-

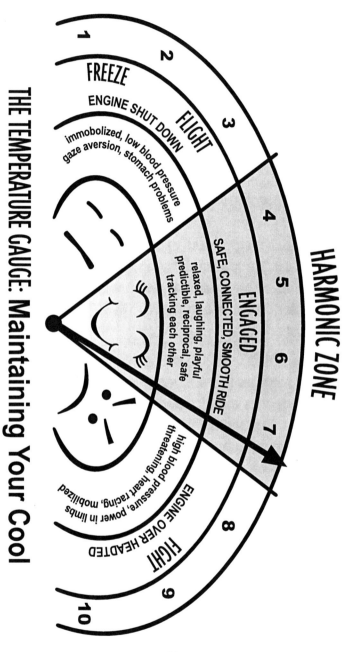

THE TEMPERATURE GAUGE: Maintaining Your Cool

HARMONIC ZONE

1 2 3 4 5 6 7 8 9 10

FREEZE

FLIGHT

ENGINE SHUT DOWN

immobolized, low blood pressure gaze aversion, stomach problems

ENGAGED

SAFE, CONNECTED, SMOOTH RIDE

relaxed, laughing, playful predictible, reciprocal, safe tracking each other

FIGHT

ENGINE OVER HEADTED

high blood pressure, power in limbs threatening, heart racing, mobilized tion." Obviously, this "shoulding" can work in your thoughts about other people too. In either case, your automatic thought is that you or someone else should/must/ought to/ has to do something.

If you notice the "car" starting to overheat, hear your "gears grinding," or sense a heavy pull, you could be in the "should" gear. The laborious lug strain on your relationship "engine" most likely indicates that your thinking is distorted.

To deal with shoulds when expectations are unrealistic of ourselves or others, change your "should" to "could" as in, "I could go to the gym" versus "I should go to the gym." It may seem simple, but coulds imply that we have a choice. Shoulds often feel like heavy obligations.

## Shifting Gears

In zone 1, 2, or 3, a person shuts down their "engine" and becomes withdrawn and immobilized. Connection has been lost, or there is not enough energy to make a good contact. One partner experiences the other as being distant, unavailable and avoidant. If you are this person, you are afraid to take your car out of the garage for fear of a collision. Fear is a weak position, so encourage yourself to turn your car on and get back on the road. Cars must be run to maintain good running order and you can't learn how to drive your car if you won't risk taking it out of the garage.

The mechanic's term for zones 4, 5, 6, and 7 is the "harmonic zone"—and it is the same in relationships. The other "too hot" or "too cold" sectors are called "friction zones"—really! The 4, 5, 6, and 7 target area promises the smoothest ride, the healthiest connection, and the best sexual relations.

Speaking of sex, there is a direct correlation between conflict done well and sexual engagement. "Emotionally nakedness" is the sparkplug that starts sexual desire. This involves sharing your deeper feelings openly and honestly without making your partner feel attacked. Start by making statements rather than asking questions, and begin these statements with "I" instead of "you." If you want stick your key in the ignition, try it!

Couples that stay in the 1, 2, or 3 range may look like they are getting along because they agree to avoid conflict. However, over time, their relationship is more like a brother and sister; there is little if any passion or sex in their relationship. They need to up the ante, risk sharing by disagreeing, and at times say what makes them angry. For these folks, anger could be a sign that they are coming alive and no longer deadening their responses.

Those who live in zone 8, 9 or 10 may surge with incredible passion at times yet burn out rapidly. Such volatility cannot be sustained. You can only race and gun your engine so long before it completely blows. These folks must find ways to de-escalate the intensity of their encounters.

Perhaps even more numerous are the combo couples; one is easily aroused (8, 9, or 10 zone) and the other is avoidant (1, 2, or 3 zone). Individuals in this "combo" situation must each take responsibility for moving into the harmonic zone.

In zones 4, 5, 6, or 7, people feel the safest to be themselves and open up to their partners, emotionally and sexually. Sex becomes a healthy and natural expression of their love for each other.

## Defensiveness

On your journey, you will be driving through many "states." Most of us hope to visit the "states" of Euphoria, Bliss, and Continual Contentment. However, you will probably have to go through the states of Confusion, Defensiveness, Anger, Boredom, and Profound Fear until you have a better navigation system.

As you become a more skilled, experienced driver and upgrade your navigational system, you will learn how to avoid spending too much time in unwanted states and spend more time in the states you prefer.

Unlike driving automobiles, defensive driving IS NOT a good idea in relationships.

> *Defensiveness is a poison pill to good relationships. In conflict, defensiveness is like blood in the water to a shark. A little here, a little there, and in no time the situation has degenerated into a feeding frenzy. Remaining non-defensive is the single most important thing you can do to increase your effectiveness when working to turn conflict into collaboration.*
> *-- Jim Tann, former judge*

## Beware or Aware?

We are either in a state of awareness or bewareness. Beware-ness says there is not enough love, money, time, status, etc. It is a weak position. Its physical symptoms may include a gnawing feeling in the stomach, adrenaline rushes, rapid, shallow breathing, restlessness, a quickened pulse, and feeling too hot or too cold.

Defensiveness is a beware state. In the long run, it is more about protecting yourself from uncomfortable feelings versus another person. Relief is only temporary, because you are engaged in distorted thinking. You are putting up armor to protect the soft part of yourself that is afraid of being hurt. At one time, this coping method may have helped with the stress of childhood—a time when you had little control over your world. As an adult, however, you are no longer at the mercy of anyone. You don't need to spend a tremendous amount of energy making sure this sensitive part doesn't get disturbed. You can experience the feelings, let the "child" part of you know that it is safe, and then respond as an adult. You can rise above these feelings and discover what is really going on. Unchecked, defensiveness becomes a burden and ultimately destroys a healthy relationship.

With awareness, you know that life is sufficient. It is the natural state of being. It is that "just noticing" place of discovery of the bigger picture. If your energies (emotions) start to move toward defensiveness, you can just watch them. You do not have to judge, fight, or feel badly about having a certain feeling. You can just notice the feeling and say, "That's interesting." You do not have to be swept away by feelings, as they are just passing through. They will move on without your needing to act on them.

## What State Are You In?

With awareness, we have much more control over our emotional states than can be imagined. At any given moment, we are either in a state of Awareness or Bewareness. Below is a chart demonstrating this principle.

| PAST | PRESENT | FUTURE |
|---|---|---|
| **Depression** | **BEWARE** | **Anxiety** |
| Stuck place: Recycling negatives or victimization without consciousness and moving forward. | Organized by fear: "The world is too big; it will not meet my needs." | Hypervigilence: Visualizing negatives |
| **Healing** | **AWARE** | **Goals** |
| Coupled with guidance: Can lead to empowerment and healing. | Consciousness: "You can do it; you can be effective. The world is sufficient to meet my needs." | Positive visualization. |

# Check Your Defensiveness Gauge

1. What are the early warning signs of defensiveness? Notice the early indicators to prevent damage to your car. Some are listed below—check the ones that are most true for you.

☐ Feeling like a victim

☐ Shutting down (complete silence)

☐ Rapid-fire talking

☐ Sudden surge of energy

☐ Sarcasm

☐ Minimizing with humor

☐ Hot or cold flashes

☐ Feeling beside yourself

☐ Arguing with "did so" and "did not" and "nuh uhh"

☐ Being inordinately contrary

☐ Seeing things as black and white

☐ Wondering why your partner is being SO ornery

2. Notice where you get stuck in your body. Is there a tightening? If so, where? Is your breathing shallow or deep? How does your stomach feel? How does your heart feel?

3. What beliefs ignite these scared feelings? Check the ones that are most true for you.

☐ I am being attacked.

☐ I am being undervalued.

☐ I am not getting enough _____.

☐ I am being abused. (What gets in the way of you using your strong part?)

☐ I am not being heard. (What is it in your beliefs or behavior that keeps you from being heard?)

☐ I am too weak to stand up for myself.

☐ I will be hurt if I am open.

4. What's the worst that could happen if you let go and did not allow yourself to be pulled into that negative vortex of energy?

5. What would happen if you just told that "little" part of yourself that everything is okay—no worries?

6. What are you afraid of losing?

If you and your partner have found yourselves in this red-hot zone, repairs are in order once you cool down.

## Lubrication

Oil fulfills some vital requirements for your engine:

- It lubricates moving parts.

- It reduces friction and wear.

- It carries away heat.

- It reduces rust and corrosion.

- It works as a seal to help prevent combustion gases from passing between the piston and cylinder walls.

### How It Works

Oil is stored in an oil pan at the bottom of the engine called the crankcase. The word works great as an analogy, because when you and or your partner get cranky, one or both of you need to splash some slippery lubricant on the situation. Oil needs to be circulating all the time to prevent you from getting cranky in the first place.

If you hear a grinding sound, you definitely need new bearings or a new way of looking at the problem.

## Oil Filter

As oil flows through the engine, it passes through an oil filter which removes abrasive particles. Over time, the filter fills up with contaminants and must be replaced at scheduled intervals.

In your relationship, you must "keep the oil clear" by getting rid of abrasive particles and contaminants—those nasty little remarks we make but don't really mean. Saying "I'm sorry" is a start. Upgrading your oil (lessening these nasty nuggets) will also help your engine run more smoothly.

*The other day I was in the local auto parts store.*
*A woman came in and asked for a seven ten cap.*
*The clerk looked perplexed. He couldn't figure out*
*what she was talking about. He asked the other*
*clerks if they knew what a 710 cap was. They all*
*scratched their heads. No one could figure it out.*
*The woman persisted. "You know, the seven ten*
*cap – it's right on the engine. Mine is missing*
*and I need a new one." "What kind of car do you*
*drive?" another guy asked (thinking that perhaps*
*she drove an old Datsun Seven Ten). The lady*
*replied, "I drive a Toyota truck." The senior clerk*
*took over. "Just how big is this cap?" he asked.*
*"About the size of my palm," she said, making a*
*circle in her hands. "Well what does it do? What*
*is it used for" asked one of the service guys. She*
*replied, I don't know, but it's always been there."*
*One of the guys gave her a note pad and asked*
*her if she could draw a picture of it. So she made*
*a circle about 3 1/2 inches in diameter and in the*
*center she wrote 710. As she was drawing, the*
*guys behind the counter looked about it upside*
*down and they fell behind the counter laughing*
*their heads off.*

## Shock Absorbers

Shock absorbers dampen the movement of the vehicle's springs as they compress and rebound during travel. Without shocks, a vehicle would continually bounce, making control difficult. Shock absorbers have a strong influence on vehicle control and handling and holds the tires to the road.

You're going to hit bumps, pits, and potholes during the journey of your relationship. How will your "car" deal with them?

What's the best shock absorber for a relationship? Humor! It is necessary for handling the jolts, jarring, and, distress of the journey.

Every couple has differences. Perhaps one thinks that good friends do not need to talk to each other and the other thinks that a lot of talk creates intimacy. One thinks that talking about problems makes them worse and the other thinks talking about problems helps to resolve them. I mean, you have a sense of humor.

You can fight about "facts" all day long. You'll end up tired, frustrated, and angry OR you could use laughter, humor, and a lighthearted attitude. Enjoy a great belly laugh at the differences between men and women. Crack up over the traits that make you interesting (or bizarre) to your spouse. Your mate's experience of the world may be amusing, at times hysterical, and at other times insightful!

 *The significant problems we have cannot be solved at the same level of thinking with which we created them. -- Albert Einstein*

You can always change your perspective and absorb the shocks of a relationship with humor.

## Alarm

A less-obvious and frequently ignored system of a car is its alarm. Your car is fitted with a sophisticated alarm system to protect the security of your car and thwart intruders who might try to steal it.

In a relationship, an intruder is someone or something outside of the couple who compromises the intimacy of the relationship. Focused care, maintenance, attention, and energy are essential to the smooth operation of your car. Sometimes the pain of a two-person relationship becomes unbearable. One or both of them may bring in a third person, place, or thing to try to relieve their pain. This forms a triangle, and your car is headed for a breakdown.

This third point is not limited to a person (a "love triangle"). It may be an activity such as sports, time on the Internet, television, or addictions.

The third point is NOT the problem. It is a symptom that one or both of the people in the relationship have given up on maintenance of their car and are spending their energy elsewhere. The car's alarm goes off when its perimeter is compromised. Sometimes, one of the partners abandons the vehicle and their partner is left "on the side of the road." If he or she mentions the alarm, it may be phrased as "It was a false alarm; nothing is wrong."

Should this unhealthy triangle continues, three distinct roles will emerge: there will be a victim, a persecutor, and a rescuer.

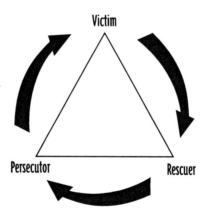

When this happens, there is little self-awareness, and each member's self-esteem is eroded. There is little opportunity for growth and what goes around comes around: you will spend time rotating through each of the roles until the triangle is destroyed. At some point, you will feel like the victim, then you will be perceived as the persecutor, and then you will feel the need to rescue or over function in this dynamic.

How do you destroy a triangle? Refocus your energy and work on the engine of your relationship. Do not allow the third party to compromise the relationship's safety. This may mean getting rid of the third point all together (as in the case of an affair or addiction); with an activity such as sports, the Internet, or television, or other activities, some of the time spent avoiding the relationship will have to be reinvested in its care.

# LOOK Under the Hood

1. What are some of the symptoms that your relationship may be getting cranky?




2. Do you schedule maintenance on a regular basis?




3. If so, who makes it happen?

4. What excuses do you make for neglecting this essential maintenance task? (Give the list of excuses here.)

5. How frequently do you laugh together? (Laughing is definitely a lubricant.)

6. When was the last time just the two of you went out and had a good time?

7. Name five other things you do to smooth and soothe your relationship on a regular basis.

# MAINTENANCE AND REPAIRS

## Maintenance

There's no such thing as a low-maintenance relationship. You can do the maintenance now or you can do it later; later is more costly.

Anything we value, we protect and take care of. There may be many reasons you value your car: it is fun, it offers status, and it gets you where you want to go. But when it comes to the care part of your treasured object, the time, expense and energy involved most often comes under the category of work.

People give me the oddest looks and comments as we discuss the "maintenance" of their relationship. The most frequent remark I hear is "It shouldn't be hard. It should be fun!" We then discuss other valued things and relationships. I don't know many individuals that find changing diapers and litter boxes fun, or cleaning the house or car enjoyable all the time, or remembering to recharge devices (cell phones, camera batteries, lap tops) in order for them to work. Then there's going to the dentist, having a mammogram or a prostate inspection, clipping our toenails, brushing our teeth, etc. Need I go on?

When we neglect to take care of something, it shows. Over time, a neglected car becomes a "clunker," and we're ready to trade it in for a new model.

At the same time, there can be great satisfaction in looking after the things that are important to us. Gratification, pride and a sense of doing something meaningful are the rewards of hard work.

## Maintenance Schedule

One of the skills for mastering maintenance is to ritualize or schedule time to do it on a regular basis. That way, you don't have to figure out or negotiate with your partner each time you need to take care of things. Rituals become habits. Over time, the maintenance just becomes a part of an ongoing routine. You know it's necessary to fuel up, change the oil in your car, and get new brakes or tires. It is an automated and accepted process of responding to the needs of things.

Carve out some special time to be together. Here are some suggestions for activities you can try.

- Take a walk.

- Take a class.

- Do a fun project.

- Take up an active hobby.

- Go bowling.

- Go dancing together.

- Try birdwatching.

- Go for a hike.

- Have a special "date" night at least once a month.

- Play board games.

- Attend religious services together.

- Check in regularly during the day.

- Recognize special days in personal ways.

- Create couple rituals throughout the year.

- Deliberately kiss or hug for one minute.

- Look each other in the eye and smile when coming or going.

Then there is the maintenance of having those necessary discussions about difficult matters and perhaps getting help from a couples' counselor to figure out why things aren't going smoothly.

At first, you must schedule these types of maintenance activities. As time goes by, and your car (relationship) responds to the benefit of regular maintenance, these rituals become automatic.

## Repairs

In your relationship, repairs counteract defensiveness, de-escalate tension and negative feeling, and reestablish goodwill after a fiery encounter. After a rough ride, you want to return to a smooth one. A repair can be a soft touch, a hug, an apology, a smile, a little humor—any attempt to lighten the tension and make you both feel more at ease. It is when you kiss and make up.

## Repair Phrases

What can you do when your relationship starts to heat up? Here are some suggested phrases for calming yourself and/or your partner.

- "My engine's flooded. Let's wait awhile before we start up this conversation again."

- "We need to slow things down."

- "When you interrupt me, I get upset because I don't feel like you are listening to me. Please let me finish."

- "Let's stop talking for a while. Just hold me."

- "This is not headed in the direction I wanted it to go. Let's stop, take a moment and talk about what's really going on."

- "I can't listen when you are yelling. Please calm down."

- "You're scaring me."

- "Let discuss this later, when the kids are in bed."

- "Neither of us is listening right now."

- "What can we do when things get this intense?"

- "I feel criticized. Would you please rephrase that?"

- "When you ask so many questions, I get defensive and flooded. Please make a statement about what's really going on with you."

- "Would you please make things more safe for me now?"

- "Whoa, slow down. Let's back up, start over, and see what's really going on."

## Tune Ups

With a car, we think we need a tune up when we have a sense that it's just not running properly or there is some kind of handling problem. Maybe it's idling rough. Maybe the timing is off. Maybe it's hard to start. Poor performance almost always means that the car needs a repair. Does the timing or tension need adjusting? Do you need new spark plugs?

A good mechanic will take time and awareness to rule out what is and isn't working. He won't just get frustrated and kick the car. When something is wrong with your car, do you hit it with a hammer and scream, "What the hell's wrong with you? Stop it!! You're a bad car!"

Yelling won't repair the car, and it won't help your relationship in any way. This is not the time to shout, "What's wrong with you? I'm talking to you! How come you won't look me in the eye when I'm trying to communicate with you!!!?"

Acting in this way is a misattribution of the problem. The problem isn't that your car (or relationship) is bad. The problem is that you want it to work but you don't know how to fix it. Blaming your partner rather than working on the issues together will only make things worse.

> Identifying the source of an error also requires knowing where and how to look. After something goes wrong, we tend to look...for the last person involved in the chain of events and blame him or her for the outcome...And systemic errors have their roots at a level above the individual.
> -- Joseph Hallinan, "Why We Make Mistakes"

In a relationship, "tuning up" means you need to tune in with and better learn how to work with your partner. Are some "repairs" in order? Do you need to make some adjustments? Notice what is and isn't working. Tune into what is really going on with your partner, and don't focus on the words or thoughts. Focus on feelings and wants instead. Better yet, tune into the eyes and body. Sharpening your awareness and just notice what is going on. In the long run, these steps will help you to tune in rather than tune out.

If you blow your engine, you'll have to take it to a mechanic, which will cost more time and money than if you took care of the problem immediately. Follow a consistent maintenance schedule rather than waiting for the "Check Engine" light.

A well-tuned car, like a healthy relationship, runs smoothly. The partners feel aligned and on the same page. They cultivate a sense of goodwill and child-like curiosity. They do the regular maintenance that creates a mutual sense of safety, security, and attraction. If things start to heat up, they can rely on each other to address problems immediately and responsibly.

# LOOK Under the Hood

## Couples Homework for Temperature Control:
## 11-Point Inspection

1. What level are you under pressure?

☐ I tend to quickly rise to an 8, 9, or 10 level.

☐ I tend to quickly withdraw to a 1, 2, or 3 level.

☐ Neither—I am always calm, cool, and collected.

2. My partner describes my behavior as:




3. The impact on my partner is:

4. The impact on my relationship is:

5. As a child, my mom under pressure was a
_____ level.

The impact on me was:

6. As a child, my dad under pressure was a
_____ level.

The impact on me was:

7. The impact on me when they engaged in conflict
was:

8. My parents split up when I was very young, so I never saw them engaging on any level.


9. My primary caregiver had multiple partners so I saw lots of stuff. The impact on me was:




10. What has made this pressure worse or better in the past?




11. Other:

# SPECIAL SITUATIONS

## The "Model" Car

I once worked with a very nice couple that had been together for 21 years. On the outside, their "car" (their relationship) looked shiny and new: the parents never argued, they took exciting family vacations together, and their kids were bright, happy, and well mannered. Add their Schnauzer, McLovin, to the mix, and they appeared to be models for a Norman Rockwell painting. At night, Mom and Dad would lovingly tuck their kids in bed and then head off to their own bed, which they shared with McLovin.

This couple did an excellent job of nurturing and maintaining their home life and relationships with their children, but they had badly neglected their marriage. They had never gone on a date that did not include their children or friends. As the years went on, the only loving that happened in their bed was stroking their dog rather than each other. They both felt the pang of emptiness in their marriage, but they ignored the "pinging" noise in their engine.

After several months of counseling, we discovered that the husband, not thinking that the car (the marriage) was going to last, had tried out a shiny new rental: another woman. (Little did he know that unless he took a drivers' education class, got a tool kit, and learned about basic maintenance, that car wouldn't last long either.)

Several weeks later, the children came to see me, their eyes frozen like a deer in the headlights. They hadn't seen this coming. Theirs was the family everyone else wanted to be like. How could Dad run off with another woman when they had never even heard an argument at home?

In the long run, the best thing you can do for your children is to keep your marriage in good working order.

# PROBLEM SITUATIONS

## Breakdowns

There are many ways that your car can break down. You can handle some of the breakdowns by yourself if you have the right equipment and information. If the damage is more serious, you'll need the help of a good mechanic. The longer you ignore the breakdown and put off going to that mechanic, the more the repairs likely will cost.

If your car break downs and you don't have roadside assistance, you may be tempted to accept help from a passing motorist. Be very careful about this as not everyone who stops to help has good intentions.

Whether it is a minor fender bender or a six-car collision, an accident is a traumatic experience and most people find it hard to think clearly, especially if someone has been seriously injured.

## People First, Property Second

Many times when people notice that their marriage is in trouble, they just keep speeding down the highway—working, caring for the kids, the house, the vehicles, the relatives. Just when the couple should pull off the road and turn on hazard lights, take a deep breath and assess the situation they put the pedal to the metal, not realizing the further damage they are doing.

When I see a couple whose marriage is in need of major repairs and yet I hear them talking about issues such as remodeling or parenting issues, I remind them that should their marriage suffer a breakdown, their problems could all end up in the hands of their attorneys. The house will be there twenty years from now, and the kids will move out and have their own lives. Without attending to the maintenance and repairs needed for their marriage, their car could eventually be a clunker headed for the junk heap.

# Flat Tires

Flat tires are a common cause of breakdowns. It is important to check the air pressure and tread of your tires on a regular basis. As usual, prevention is better than break downs. If you have a blowout, the popping sound and sudden sagging to one side of your car will tell or, less dramatic, flip flop sound will let you know you've gone flat. In either case, take your foot off the gas, let the car slow down and pull off the road.

How do you know when you have a flat tire in your relationship? Your relationship is flat when it lacks the positive energy and enthusiasm necessary for a smooth ride. The flatness could be due to apathy, depression, or constant criticism and nit picking (these are like punctures); lightness and buoyancy are missing. It's time to inflate to the proper tire pressure.

Many couples that face a flat tire in their relationship continue on, full speed ahead, without stopping to address the problem. Some of the phrases I commonly hear from these couples include the following:

- "She always /never does such and such."

- "I feel taken for granted."

- "I've heard this all before."

Are you prepared for a flat in your relationship? Without realizing that flat tires sometimes happen, and how to fix them, you may waste time blaming each other for the breakdown as opposed to making the repair.

How can a couple with a flat tire fix their problem?

Slow down and pull well off the road and onto a level area if possible. Put the car in park, and apply the parking brake.

Slow down from all outside activities—work, the kids, doing housework or yard work. Take time out to go on a date away from the demands of home, job, kids, and pets.

**Take out the spare tire, the jack, and the lug wrench. Take off the hubcap and loosen the lug nuts.**

Take a minute to look into what has happened. Be prepared to loosen your attachment to being right, blaming, and negative expectancy.

**Jack up the car and put on a spare.**

Elevate the relationship to the place it deserves instead of trying to drive full speed ahead when things seem a little flat. Go on a date, inflate each other and pump up the four tires of your relationship: appreciation, curiosity, fun, and positive expectancy.

Your tires need a certain amount of tire pressure for optimal functioning. Check your tires on a regular basis to make sure they are properly inflated!

# EMERGENCIES

A collision may affect those involved for years after the cars have been towed away and repaired—especially if someone was permanently disabled or killed. Accidents shake up your confidence. Sometimes, it may be difficult to get in a car ever again.

Any event that causes a serious separation, such as death and divorce, is emotionally jarring. Partners in a marriage should NEVER threaten each other with divorce unless there is immediate intention. I tell my clients that if someone threatens to divorce their partner, the next call needs to be to an attorney. If they threaten death (suicide or homicide), the next call needs to be to the police. And these conversations should NEVER take place around children of any age.

Passengers to such threats are in for a terrifying ride. They are now hostages to feelings of help-lessness, alarm, angst. In the case of suicide, it is important for passengers to know that no one can keep someone intent on committing suicide from doing so. Once again, get professional help.

How do you know when the situation is urgent or something you can't fix yourself? You've gotten off course and are headed for a terrible (if not fatal) collision when the three "A's" are involved: Abuse, Addiction, or Affairs.

Learn healthy ways to maintain your relationship rather than crashing the car.

# LOOK Under the Hood

## If you are causing emergencies situations mentioned ask yourself:

1. How has abuse, addiction, an affair, or other threatening behaviors caused you trouble?

2. What is the impact on your partner, children, extended family, friends, work, and finances?

3. If you continue this sabotaging behavior, what will be the impact on everyone ten days, ten months, and ten years from now?

4. What steps can you take this week to actively deal with your problem?

# RESPONSIBLE DRIVING

## Braking and Acceleration

When some couples hit a "bumpy" or "slippery" place in their relationship, the tension compels one or both to "accelerate" and increase the intensity, even to the point where the intensity (the accelerator pedal) seems stuck. Some drivers are in a constant state of road rage. Little things bug them A LOT!! They are impatient, irritated, angry, and demanding. It's like they are always accelerating and their gas pedal is always stuck.

In this case, slowing down and "pulling off to the side of the road" is the most effective way to manage the "acceleration."

In a relationship, sudden and extreme acceleration feels out of control and scary, and it can lead to a rapid deterioration of the relationship. Remember to take your foot off the accelerator and put on the brakes.

# Driven to Distraction Sexting, Texting, Cybersex, and other E-lationships

An "e-lationship" is one where much of the communication or correspondence happens via a device. These people won't make the time to show up in person yet spend much of their time "connecting" through e-mail, mobile phones, texts, tweets, IMs, chat rooms, or social networking sites, etc.. They think they are communicating and having conversations but are actually avoiding all their senses. On the road, these distractions can be deadly.

Just as cell phones, radios, MP3 players, the GPS, and many other devices can take our focus off the road and cause an accident, the same is true in relationships. Couples who have important conversations over these devices are missing sensory cues such as touch, voice, and sight, not to mention the energetic field between the couple. And eye contact is essential for meaningful communication.

I've come across couples who fight by means of texting. They are fexting. They recount the blow-by-blow frames of a recent fight with their partner, and they think it is important for me to analyze each word on the screen. I no longer look at text messages but instead tell the frenzied fexters that words on a screen are meaningless. They carry no sensory data, no sounds or non-verbal cues.

Then I tell these couples that if they continue fexting, they must do sexting through text only as opposed to actual sex. No takers yet!

Devices are poor substitutes for the real thing.

It's mind-boggling what modern technology can do. It can make our lives easier, more efficient, and even more connected if we use it effectively. Is technology good or bad? It depends upon how you use it.

Intentionality comes to mind. What is your intention when you are in the car? If you are serious about driving well (having a great relationship) you will do your e-lating cautiously.

Here are some healthy ways to use technology to connect:

- Texting SHORT phrases to your partner (e.g., "ILY").

- Using Skype to web conference with partners who are temporarily dislocated (in a war zone or on a business trip).

When NOT to use e-lating:

- To have serious discussions

- To have on-going fights

- To break up

- To scare or threaten suicide

In a rich and fulfilling union with your beloved, you are unaware of anything outside of your partner— the touch, smell, the taste of lips, the murmuring of the voice, the look in the eyes. How do these compare to cyberspace?

In the presence of our partner, we are weaving together states of consciousness heading for a common destination: ecstatic connection. Those undulating unbound waves are created in each other's presence. You are actually changing each other's chemistry and brain functioning.

Internet porn and vibrators may be satisfying on some level, but using them is a solitary, self-focused activity. You are not exchanging that amazing sexual energy with your lover. In the presence of your partner, hormones are released that help you bond with each other. The presence of each other soothes and opens your heart.

 *Out beyond ideas of wrong doing and right doing, there is a field. I will meet you there. When the soul lies down in that grass, the world is too full to talk about. Ideas, language, even the phrase each other doesn't make sense.*
*-- Rumi*

# Defensiveness

Being defensive takes a tremendous amount of work. You must put up armor and protect the soft part of yourself that might be hurt by another. You close off a valve to your heart. You spend so much energy making sure that this sensitive part isn't hurt that you lose your access to it completely.

When energies start to move, you don't have to go there. When people totally lose control, they have allowed their beliefs to control them. They have given a passing thought or feeling way too much attention.

Just notice your thoughts and beliefs. Don't judge, or fight, or feel badly for having certain feelings. Just notice them and say, "That's interesting." This ability to quickly reclaim your center is a valuable skill in relationships.

According to Dr. John Gottman, having an effective way to manage anxiety is one of the four basic factors of a happy marriage. The other three are love, a common vision and commitment.

# Driving Under the Influence

Your brain is similar to the automatic transmission of a car. It consists of many parts and systems that work together in a delicate symphony of amazing mechanical and electrical functions. It controls the body and every move it makes as well as all thought and action. It is the center of the human nervous system.

Drugs and alcohol diminishes these functions. It

distorts emotions, memory, impulse control, alertness, inhibitions and judgment. Excessive and addictive users lose interest in many areas of life, including school, sports, family, and friends.

People who drink alcohol then drive a car choose to drive with a diminished brain capacity critical to responsible driving. They cannot fully respond to the requirements at hand. Passengers do not feel safe in the car.

Being able to respond with a fully functioning brain is just as essential to relationships as it is to driving a car. The number of accidents, divorces, and families injured by drunken drivers is phenomenal.

What are the effects of alcohol abuse on marital satisfaction and quality?

# The Designated Driver

When alcohol abuse is involved in a relationship communication becomes more negative, hostile, blaming, or nonexistent. The couple's problem solving ability is compromised. The maintenance and repairs necessary to sustain a marriage or family deteriorate. Often one partner becomes the designated driver shouldering the burdensome responsibility of not only driving the car alone but tending to damages done by the drunk driver as well.

Adult alcohol abuse creates additional social, emotional, behavioral, and academic problems for the couple's children as well. The home is no longer a warm, welcoming place to bring friends. Both the spouse and the children are constantly concerned about what unpredictable behavior will happen next. With all the tension fighting, will the car be totaled?

There is also an increasing amount of violence in families with addicted adults. [See section on Road Rage.]

Then there is the matter of sexual intimacy; who wants to who wants to make love to a stinky, sloppy drunk? Alcohol impairs performance and keeps one from being fully emotionally present.

In marriages with addiction problems, the warmth, unity and goodwill necessary for the smooth ride disappear. **Marital satisfaction doesn't stand a chance with this amount of toxic tension.**

Divorced or separated men and women are three times more likely to be alcoholics or to have an alcohol problem than are married men and women.

Therefore, when a couple comes to me and wants to discuss the fight they had last week while "under the influence" or inebriated I ask, "How could it be any other way? You gave up the awareness and control necessary for useful communication and for steering your relationship in the proper direction. I cannot teach you how to drive under the influence."

"Under the influence" also applies to other addictions that take time, money, energy, resources, and emotional presence away from the relationship. These include but are not limited to street drugs, misuse of prescription drugs, gambling, extreme overeating, the Internet, and television.

**No relationship is low maintenance.** One needs to show up, be present, and respond to that which they say is valuable.

## Aggressive Driving and Road Rage

There is a direct correlation between road rage and domestic violence. Both happen because an individual allows anger to escalate to dangerous levels then uses the car as a container to express anger without consideration of the passengers, the well-being of the car and other drivers. Clearly, "rage" is a matter of degree and not all anger is uncontrolled or even inappropriate. How a person responds to anger is what matters.

Road rage most often comes from a place of self-righteous entitlement and lack of time, impatience, and poor impulse control. It is exceedingly confrontational. People showing road rage act out with their car in ways they never would in another setting without consideration for their passengers or the community.

On the road, how can you best deal with road rage?

1. Don't retaliate. Never take the other driver's actions personally.

2. Don't make eye contact with an angry driver.

3. Before you jump out to challenge the other driver, ask yourself, "Is throwing this tantrum worth risking a fight?"

4. Be polite and courteous, even when others are not.

5. Always ask yourself, "Could the other driver have possibly made a mistake?"

6. If you are harassed by another driver and feel in eminent danger, call the police.

7. Remain calm and relaxed.

8. Never underestimate the other driver's capacity for mayhem.

9. Allow enough time to get where you are going.

10. Remember that you cannot control the drivers around you, but you can control your own reaction.

   A wide range of actions are included in the catch-all phrase of road rage. Many of the actions are minor and related to low levels of frustration whereas some are more severe and relate more to assault or criminal action.

| Actions associated with road rage include the following: | In a close relationship, "road rage" may erupt as one or more of the following: |
|---|---|
| Beeping the horn | Yelling/name calling |
| Pursuing a vehicle | Backing someone into a corner |
| Flashing head lights | Making threatening gestures |
| Forcing a car off the road | Shoving/restraining |
| Verbal Abuse | Name calling |
| Bumping into another car | Using sarcasm/contempt/ humiliation |
| Tailgating | Following too closely |
| Threatening another driver | Threats to hurt partner/children/ extended family pets |
| Braking or slowing suddenly | |
| Intentionally damaging another vehicle | Throwing things/smashing doors or walls |
| Cutting off or swerving in front | Cutting off partner from friends, support system/isolation |
| Deliberate obstruction | Blocking to prevent leaving a room |
| Physically assaulting another driver | Throwing things, smashing doors or walls/pushing, shoving, beating/push, shove, strangle, jerk, slap, shake, bruise, kick, punch, hit |
| Use of weapons | Use of weapons |

These are problems that the two of you will not resolve on your own. Calling a mechanic (a marriage counselor) or specialty shop is essential. "Specialty shops" can include such programs as anger management, DAWN (Domestic Violence for Women's Network), or specific 12-step programs.

# RESPONSIBLE OWNERSHIP

## Detailing Your Car

Detailing your car not only makes it look good, also it increases its value and makes for a much more pleasant ride. Take the time to make it look shiny and new:

- Give it a wash and wax

- Clean the windows

- Repair dings, dents, and rust spots

- Tidy up the interior

- Tidy up under the hood

- Touch up the paint

Doesn't riding around in your freshly groomed car give you a feeling of pride?

For couples, here are a few ways to "detail your car".

- Bathe together

- Massage each other

- Look for new perspectives

- Randomly apologize or do a kind deed to make up for an old hurt

- Other-

You will be amazed at how good it feels to attend to the small details of your relationship and keep it looking as beautiful as the day you drove it off the lot.

# THE ROAD AHEAD

On the road trip of your life, you may see breath-taking vistas, stunning landscapes, historical attractions, picturesque small towns on scenic back roads, and fun-filled cities. You will recycle these memories over and over as a part of a rich history the two of you have created together.

Don't be surprised if the stories you tell over and over again with the most exuberance are the ones in which the two of you overcame adversity.

"Remember the time we ran out of gas in a blizzard on the mountain pass and barely made it to a gas station?" Do you recall how you conquered that "near death" experience?

A marriage really is about the journey and sharing it with that special someone as you grow and change.

HOW you respond to the incredible amount of changes that will happen will determine how successful you are as a couple. There will be happy, exciting adventures and events you could have never imagined.

With increasing awareness of how to care for your car and willingness to take the time to invest in its maintenance and repairs, it not only will take you far but it can be a good ride. In the long run, something valued increases in value. At the end of the day, your relationship will be something that you will be proud of.

Take care of your car, and your car will care for you.

*The road to success is always under construction.*
*-- Lily Tomlin*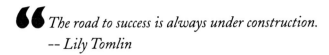

## Expectations

The quality of your joint journey will be determined by your expectations and how you tell the story of what happened.

Learn to take it in stride when things go wrong. You've done your best to be prepared, to take driving instruction, and to be sure that the necessary tools are handy. To make this point, I was inspired by that great read of Dr. Seuss entitled Oh the Places You'll Go to write the following:

*There will be great days when you'll be cruising along,*

*You're babe at your side, and a drive along song*

*You're gleeful, content and indeed you're most happy.*

*You're feeling so good, it is downright quite sappy.*

*Yet on a long journey, things can happen and do.*

*Don't be surprised when bad things happen to you.*

*There's no one to blame; no one is bad.*

*Breakdowns, bad weather, getting lost make you sad.*

*Tension, frustration may be a part of the course.*

*Don't snap at your partner, that is not the source.*

## Telling the Story

How you tell the story is more important than what happened.

Was it "We got lost and it as awful!" OR "We got lost, but in trying to find our way back to the freeway, we discovered this park with a waterfall so we decided to take a break and have a picnic lunch".

"We had a flat on route to Reno, and it ruined our trip." OR "We had a flat, but had the tools and spare tire to fix it. We were back on the road in no time at all."

In fact, have you ever noticed how some stories change as they get told over and over? Consciously change your life stories for the better. Give more air-time to the divine and less to the disaster. Then this becomes the new "memory" of the trip.

At the end of your journey, the focus of your shared adventure and ultimate shared history will determine its value.

Take care of the car—then hang on for a wonder-filled ride.

# STATE OF AWARENESS

## Universal Learner's Permit

## You are now a card-carrying learner.

**This card allows you to:**

1. Not know everything until you are a certified driver. [Just because you may be certifiable does not mean you are certified.]

2. Until then you are humbly reassured that you are entitled to:

   a. Make mistakes

   b. Fail: it is a learning process

   c. Model imperfection

   d. Own imperfection, apologize and make repairs when necessary

**Your permit may be suspended if you:**

1. "Should" on yourself (no "shoulding" allowed)

2. Try to be an imposter of perfection and flawness performance

3. Try to use it in any other state other than Awareness

4. Try to drive under the influence

5. Engage in reckless driving

6. If you cause an accident and fail to make repairs

**PRACTICE**  **PRACTICE**

**PRACTICE**

Connie Bellemere, MA,
Licensed Mental Health Counselor

Connie has a remarkable career as a counselor with twenty years of experience. She is an award-winning speaker and has been a technical consultant for a Warner Brothers television series.

She is passionate about bringing curiosity, fun, and simplicity to her work with couples. Her trademark "car talk," clarity, and wit offer an innovative and disarming approach, but don't let its simplicity fool you. Her counseling practice weaves together the cutting-edge methods of John Gottman, PhD, and Stan Tatkin, expert in the psychobiology of couples counseling.

Connie lives in the Puget Sound area, surrounded by a tapestry of family, friends, and the enchanting, evergreen outdoors. While she delights in walk-abouts, hiking, tennis, and dancing, she relishes just "being" with those she loves.

Information about her practice can be found at www.soundcounseling.net.